I0419819

# Holidays and Travel

# Safety and Travel Tips for Women

**Dueep Jyot Singh**

**Mendon Cottage Books**

*JD-Biz Publishing*

Our books are available at

1. Amazon.com

2. Barnes and Noble

3. Itunes

4. Kobo

5. Smashwords

6. Google Play Books

# Table of Contents

# Introduction

The 21$^{st}$ century has given rise to a number of clichés, among which the world has gotten smaller is a popular one. And this is because of the rise in methods of transport, with which we can zip from one corner of the earth to the other, with lots of ease and with just a hitch of our carpet bags on our shoulders.

Once upon a time, just going outside your city walls are your city limits and boundaries was fraught with peril. One never knew whether you would come back again safely, because you were going into strange territory. And it was always the menfolk who tried this brave adventure into the unknown. The womenfolk stayed at home.

However, as time went by, womenfolk also began to get more peripatetic, especially if you read about the Widow of Bath in Chaucer's Canterbury Tales, who was on a pilgrimage to Canterbury and had managed to visit Jerusalem, in those medieval times! She must have been a really brave and intrepid soul to have embarked on such an adventure in such lawless times.

The 21$^{st}$ century may be more law-abiding, but even then, a single woman going off all on her own, on her ownsome is a safety hazard. In most cases, she may go off and survive her trip without any wrinkles or tough spots, but on the other hand, there is a chance that she may face some problems – physical and mental, just because she is a woman on her own.

This book is going to give you a lot of tips and techniques, based on my experience as a peripatetic female traveling alone all over the compass, as well as common sense tips, which can help add to your safety. Especially when you are a single woman traveling to an unknown or unknown spot on the globe, all alone.

# Holidays and Traveling All Alone

Holidays can be a challenging time, especially for singles, but with proper planning and a sensible outlook, you can use this time to discover brand-new vistas in life. Holidays can be a time for a new beginning and they can teach you how to be at peace with yourself and the world.

Someone asked me why I preferred going all alone on holidays, instead of taking my family along with me. Was I not afraid? Many people were surprised when they saw a permanent bag packed in my bedroom, which meant that I could travel anywhere, at any time. Many people are not so fortunate to have that sort of chance in their lives.

But having a job, which entailed a lot of touring, it meant that I would be given orders at night to catch the morning flight to XYZ to attend some important meeting, take up some training sessions or even interview, future candidates for our training programs.

I did not worry much about my safety, because there were three points which worked in my favor. I knew where I was going. I knew how I was going to get there, and I knew that there was a roof and a shelter waiting for me at my destination.

So let us look at the first point –

## Knowledge of Where You Are Going

If you are going to a place that you know very well, you know that you are comparatively safe. But if you are going to a destination where you have not been before, it is better to arm yourself with knowledge about that place beforehand.

Do some research. Only fools walk in where angels fear to tread, and a woman traveling alone has to be practical and sensible, instead of acting like an irresponsible and possibly helpless fool.

Learn the route from the airport to your destination. Look at the landmarks, when you are traveling to that particular place. But do not look at them so eagerly so that your driver decides that you are a tourist, gawking at the wonders of his city and thus a pigeon to be plucked. He may definitely want to take you by the longer route, so that the fare meter runs up.

I remember going to a strange city for the first time, and my official hosts had told me that the office and the place where I was to stay was just half a mile away from the airport. When I asked them the way to get there, I noted down the roads. After that, I asked whether there was a longer route taking me to that particular destination and the secretary giving me this information giggled, when I explained to her that taxi services normally took the longer route to a destination which was quite near.

She found that interesting. And believe it or not, that is what happened. I got off the plane, hailed a taxi and asked him to take me to our office. The moment he turned towards the longer route, I growled at him. What did he think he was doing? I wanted him to take ABC road. Why was he going the roundabout way? All in the local vernacular.

He gave a feeble grin and got me to my destination within 10 minutes. And then he paid me the ultimate accolade – ma'am, I did not know that you belonged to the city. I thought you were a tourist!"

Knowledge of how to get there is the second point.

## Getting There

You need to be familiar with all the transport methods taking you to your destination and away from it. I remember going on an official tour to one of the disturbed areas, which was under military curfew. But as I had military escort, and I was on official duty, I was not bothered much about getting there and coming back.

Nevertheless, even with my travel plans made for me by my hosts, I make sure that I knew all about how to get out of that place in an emergency.

Why did I need to do this? This was if I missed my plane, due to any sort of reason, the only way to get out of that place would have been to catch a bus, travel throughout the night for 12 hours through mountainous, potential rock falls, and terrorist infested areas and reach the capital city. From there, one could catch a train to wherever one wished to go.

Luckily, I did not miss the plane back. But I knew that just in case the plane did not land due to weather problems or was canceled due to political turmoil, especially with   insurgency rampant in that area, I could get out by road. I could even hire a taxi or a car to take me wherever I wanted to go.

So remember to have all your escape routes well at hand, and easily accessible. Because who knows you may need to use them as a last resort. And lastly, do not be like me, going off in areas which are political bombshells. This sort of irresponsible behavior may be all right when one is young and is not very much bothered about mortality or is too stupid to imagine what could happen possibly if the world blew up in one's face, but age brings with it wisdom! So do not take any foolish chances, especially in this day and age!

## Shelter for You

I think the nicest thing about journeys, traveling and trips is when you have reach your destination, and plumped yourself on your bed, take off your shoes and thrown them at the nearest wall. If you have a house to go to, when you are traveling, you do not have to worry, because after all, you are going to your own shelter. But if you have staying in a hotel, remember to book ahead.

Look for women friendly hotels. Some hotels may have special rooms which are designed with the female traveler in mind. These rooms are stocked with irons, hair driers, and such necessary equipment, so that you can avoid calling room service. Make sure that the rooms are in a safe location. They should not be down a long hallway or facing a deserted carpark.

You may also want to find rooms with kitchen facilities. This is so that you can avoid going out to eat, or eating alone in restaurants. It also helps to save money!

## Where art Thou?

I remember going on a family trip in the 80s with my father and my brother. We were trekking from Srinagar to Leh, on foot, just for adventure, through some of the most lonesome, potentially dangerous and godforsaken areas on planet Earth. You could go 200 miles without seeing a human, or even anything living. So of course there was no question of any hotels around to provide us with necessary food. But we did not care. We had bread, cheese, salad leaves, a packet of ham, tomatoes, salt-and-pepper, and Swiss pen knives in our rucksacks. No worry about food!

It took us 22 days to do this trek of 159.7 miles, via Kargil and the dangerous passes of Zojhi-La and Fotu-La. But we kids were still teenagers then and very energetic. Nevertheless, whenever I think about this bit of very foolish daredevilry now, I shudder. We were three innocent simpletons, who did not even know about the inherent dangers of going through unknown land without any medium of communication.

Nobody knew where we were. Nobody knew our destination. All our relatives knew that we were traveling somewhere in Kashmir, for the holidays. And if we never returned from those holidays, nobody would know where to find us! Because we were somewhere near Kargil and Dras when everyone was possibly hunting for us in Srinagar.

So take my advice. Let people know where you are. Do not be reckless and foolhardy like we Three Musketeers, even though we had an adult to take care of us. But father himself was the intrepid sort of globe trotter who was quite capable of going everywhere without bothering about what would happen or what could happen. And he passed on those reckless and traveling genes to his kids.

And father having gone through 30 countries or more without a scratch or a wince was definitely not going to worry about a teeny-weeny trip in the mountains of Ladakh.

You had better be more sensible. Keep a cell phone with you. Have your GPS tracking on. Make sure the cell phone is charged every night. Also keep a pen and paper handy to write notes in an emergency.

# Women Friendly Tours

More and more travel agencies are offering women friendly tours to their clients. Not only are these comparatively safe, but many professional women use these trips as a mode of relaxation, as well as networking! These holidays are going to include adventure travel, as well as spa holidays.

These are the most popular choices of women, when they are having with other women.

You may also want to ensure that these travel agencies book you in compartments which have been reserved for women. These are common in France and in Spain. They are also available in many parts of the East. You are going to be comparatively safe in these travel coupes, where your travel companions are going to be women.

Even though these are not totally safe. I do not know whether I am incident – prone, or things just happen to me, but each trip that I take teaches me something new, especially about the people I meet.

So I was traveling on an overnight journey, in one of these reserved for women coupes. The occupant of the berth next to mine was getting off at about two in the morning at her destination, while I would be reaching my destination at about nine in the morning.

She spent all the time asking me inquisitive questions about me, my family, my background, and other matters, consisting of Small talk, in many parts of the world. I used all my creative efforts to spin her really tall tales about myself and my antecedents.

At about 2 o'clock, I felt a tug at the bag underneath my head. She was approaching her destination and had decided to make her journey more productive by purloining my luggage. I opened one drowsy eye, and hooted sleepily, "do not bother, "aunty", I have chained my bag to the seat."

She gave a half embarrassed titter, muttered something about not knowing where she was in the dark, and disappeared into the gloaming. I had done that with my bag as well as with the suitcase, so when you are traveling, you can add a couple of luggage chains, to secure your bags.

Do not talk about yourself and especially do not give your address to anybody who is hail fellow well met. Do you give your phone number and address to strangers in your own city? You do not do you? So why do you want to do that when you are abroad?

However, if you have made some really genuine friends, you may just want to give your address to them in case they want to get in touch with you. But in most cases, these addresses get packed in memory boxes and gather dust.

Let me tell you something about cruises. Now that travel agencies know that I am a peripatetic person, they keep sending me invitations to go on a cruise, the experience of a lifetime, and all that jazz. Let me tell you something about cruises.

If you are a single person traveling, you may have to pay a large sum of money extra. This is some sort of penalty. So I would suggest, that if you want to go on a cruise, just be on the lookout for last-minute cancellations. Nip in there and book your cabin.

This last-minute deal means that they are going to agree to waive that extra fee just because they want to fill in the empty cabin. I normally call the cruise lines directly, and ask them if they have any last minute cancellations. Royal Caribbean cruises based in Miami is offering you interesting package tours and also the chance to win in a competitions throughout the year.

But I would suggest, if you want to go on a cruise, you can ask your favorite travel agent for the best deals, he can give you. I remember one of my friends, who worked in the city's most well-known travel agency, before she joined our organization as a faculty member. I intended to book my tours from this agency, but I desisted, the moment I found out the way the employees were treated by their penny-pinching boss.

Every month, when he had to pay them their salaries, he used to call them to his room, and then begin asking them about the number of clients they had booked that month, and tick off their names with a "you did not manage to persuade that person to book on that tour, through your own sales tactics, because he is my friend and he booked this tour to do me a favor."

And thus, with these excuses, he managed to dock their salaries, because *they did not deserve it.* No wonder she left after eight months. But as I am not selling package tours, but I am more interested in the safety aspects of group vacations for women, here are some suggestions.

# Tips for Group Vacations

If the thought of spending your holidays all alone, is overwhelming, you can try group vacations. These tours/vacation packages which are designed for single people, you can consider this to be a really great and enjoyable option.

Apart from meeting people with similar interests, you just might not have to worry about a solo vacation again. But do not plan to spend the entire holiday season with people in your group. Supposing your holiday is for one month, spend about two weeks or three weeks in a group vacation. Leave one week for yourself.

If you are not the extrovert-ish kind, you may find the presence of all these people to be rather claustrophobic and overwhelming. Seriously, I have never taken a group vacation, because I just cannot bear the close proximity of a group bound to a fixed timetable. And also an itinerary.

This reminds me of one of my favorite jokes told to me by my father about some travelers who decided to visit Italy for their vacation. They drove up to Pompeii in the morning, and the moment they reached there, they looked at their itinerary. "Poppa," says the woman, "we visited the wrong place today, this was scheduled for tomorrow." "You are right, momma," said her spouse, and they drove back to their hotel right then.

That is the reason why I do not like itineraries! Also, the problem with group tours is that many of them do not allow you to go out all alone, exploring the city.

However, if you are in a group tour, you may want to seek out other single tourists, with whom you can feel relaxed. Do not impose yourself on the other members of your group, unless you are invited. Find places which are going to stimulate and amuse you. These include local areas, where it is safe for women to go, and other points of interest.

Whenever I go to a new city, after I have done my research on it, I make sure that I get on good and friendly terms with the employees in the hotel. I always asked the receptionist if she could recommend me the best place to go eat, visit, shop, or just walk.

Naturally, there are many people, who are very pleased to give you all this information. You may also want to ask them any points of etiquette or social behavior, about which you have to be careful in order not to offend the sensibilities of the locals.

For example, if you are in Thailand, never, ever touch anybody on the head. We are so used to patting children on the heads in a patronizing manner, but you never do it when you are in Thailand.

In the same way, if you are in the East, never praise a child in front of its parents, by exclaiming about its beauty or its intelligence. God forbid if the child falls sick, you are going to be blamed for casting an evil eye upon it! Believe it or not, these ancient superstitions still prevail in the mind and psyche of even people who are supposed to be educated, cultured and sophisticated.

# Planning for your trip

I normally take just one long holiday every year, and half of the fun is planning for it and looking forward to it. So remember to plan your trip for our after peak times. You can easily chop the cost of your air and lodging when you go on a tour in the off-season period. Also, you are going to find the lodgings as well as the tourist spots less crowded.

I remember taking my father on a trip to a very well-known and expensive hill station, as his birthday present about a decade ago. As his birthday was in September, this was the off-season. So father was lodged in superb five star hotels at one eighth the cost of what I would have to pay, if we had to come visit in the peak season of May to August. Naturally he enjoyed his birthday present very much.

Apart from that, he did not need to bother about restaurant reservations, for dining out. As there were nearly no tourists, all I did was drag them into my favorite restaurant, whenever he was hungry, and he would have a table available for him without much Ado. This does not happen very often in the peak season.

So naturally, my trips are planned in September/October before the cold winter sets in. Financial planning is half of the fun, and this I learned from my father, when I was very young. He talked about young Australian miners, he had seen working in Mount Newman. These Husky young men worked day and night for six months in grueling conditions and saved all their money. And then they left their jobs to spend all their money in riotous living, in Sydney, Adelaide and Perth for the next six months!

And when their money was finished, they came back and picked up their mining jobs again! And because these experienced men were very much in demand, they were welcomed back after their spending binge.

So my holidays are my spending binge. I figure out what 20% of my net salary is. Net is what is written on your salary check, after the tax deductions and other deductions! Save it methodically, every time you get paid. Sometimes I do a little bit of cheating, and when I go shopping, and get tempted with something which looks attractive, but is of no early use, I ask its price. Then I go and put that amount in my holiday fund. Incidentally, by the time I come back home, I usually forget about that thing which looked so attractive and was so expensive and so utterly useless. This helps fill my fund even faster!

Do this saving every time you get your check. Or you may set up a payroll deduction from your accounts department, to make sure that all that money is going straight into your savings account automatically.

Keep the savings account, apart from your salary savings account. You take out the money for your daily and monthly expenses from your normal salary savings account, do not you. Your holiday savings account has to be a thing apart. You are not going to touch it except when you are withdrawing money to buy your plane tickets!

Use 10% of this money for equipping yourself for your journey including clothes, good shoes, medicines and other necessary items. Another 10% is going to be kept for emergencies. The rest of the money can be utilized for traveling, and other related activities. By doing this you do not have to rely upon your credit cards or even loans for the things you want to do, or buy.

# Bank Balances

Talking about bank balances. When you are traveling, make sure that you have enough of money left in your bank and easily accessible, so that you can get back home safely. This money should be enough for a plane ticket, as well as enough to pay your hotel bills.

A couple of months ago, a friend of mine, went on a holiday to Turkey. Her flight back was to take place the next morning, so she decided to do some last-minute shopping before her flight. That decision proved fatal to her purse, as well as her money belt, which had her passport and all the necessary papers, which soon became the property of a pickpocket.

She was in dire straits. No money, no passport no plane tickets. Apart from that, she could not get out of her hotel until she had paid her bill. And her flight was three hours away. She immediately did what she could, she emailed everyone on her mailing list asking whether they could send her some money via Western Union!

I opened up my mail too late to send her some money – she needed an equivalent of $1000 to pay her hotel bill and more for a plane ticket. I wondered what she would do for a passport!

Now here are the mistakes she made. She took all her papers along with her when shopping. She left her shopping for the last minute, when she should have been packing and getting ready to go to the airport. She did not have enough of money as a backup, in her room, to pay her hotel bill and to pay for her taxi to the airport.

I wonder why she thought she needed to take her passport and her plane tickets along with her money to the market when going shopping. If I were her, I would have placed them in the hotel's safe, if I thought my hotel room was not secure enough.

Also, she did not have enough of money in her bank to pay for her dues and she had to fall on the bounty of all the people on her email address book list! How many of us must have thought cynically that this was a sell and why should we send any money to someone we knew superficially? How many of us must have prided ourselves on the fact that we would not make any such silly mistake, when we went traveling.

I still wonder how she got back. Because since that day. I have not heard from her. I think she was offended because I did not send her any money. Well, enemies do not believe your explanations, friends do not need them!

So remember, have plenty of money ready at hand for emergencies.

# Medical Insurance and Language

Is it necessary for you to take out medical insurance when you are traveling? I would suggest, that you do that, especially if you are traveling abroad. God forbid, if you meet with an accident, and are in a country where the medical costs are prohibitive, you are going to find your money, clean wiped out just in paying the medical bills.

A colleague's brother took his family to Paris on a trip. And he fell sick there. He was immediately taken to the hospital. He had no medical insurance. Luckily, he had a credit card and a healthy bank balance back home.

The trip was cut short when he was stabilized, and could come back home. The next morning my friend brought his credit card to me, and told me to talk to the people in the hospital for payment through credit card – in French.

I remember trying to persuade an irate and impatient woman that the number of the credit card was right, though she kept telling me Madame, you are telling me the wrong number.[1] the payment cannot be done through this credit card." Finally, I had to tell her, if she knew English and could understand the numbers, if spoken in English. And then I spoke the numbers to her, one by one, in English! The bill was about 3000 Euros.

And so the bill was paid.

---

[1] Incidentally, she was very rude and very impatient.

But I think if I had trouble communicating with her in a language which I spoke and knew well, I wonder how my friend's brother who just knew English had managed to survive on a trip to a place where he did not know the language, or could get himself understood, especially in an emergency.

How many of us go to Spain, France, and other places where " English is not spoken", without even bothering to learn the local language? I did not face this problem very often, because I have been multilingual since childhood, and picked up languages very easily, thanks to a cosmopolitan and peripatetic upbringing. So that is why I could not understand why people did not learn the local language when they went to a new place.

At least they should have learned some basics. How to ask for directions, order food, and negotiating prices in the markets (thus avoiding getting taken advantage of).

So remember, I would suggest you go to places where you know the language well, and you can communicate to them, especially when you are sick or you need the help of the police. As for medical insurance, even if you are going on a small trip, it is better to have somebody else picking up the medical bills.

Funnily enough, all the time I had medical insurance, I never needed it. However, the moment my medical insurance expired, and I was a bit too tardy about renewing it, I went on a trip and came down with sunstroke plus botulism! Luckily enough, I did not have to be hospitalized, otherwise I would have to pay, heaven knows how much money from my own pocket.

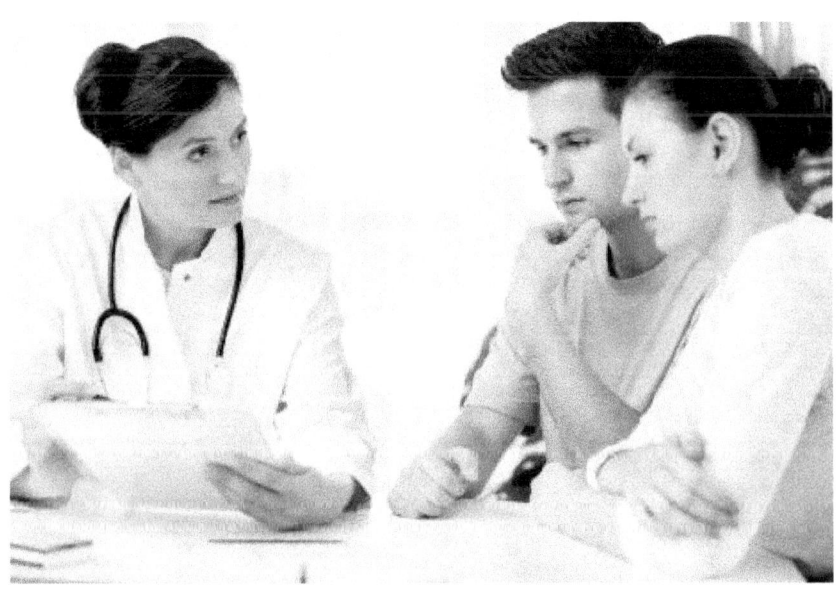

---

This reminds me – you would want to see your doctor before you go on a trip. Ask him for medicines, if you are taking some medication. And if you feel airsick and seasick, here is one natural remedy, which you may want to try out. This is my own recipe which works wonderfully well for me and my other peripatetic friends

Take one teaspoonful of ginger, the juice of one lemon, one teaspoonful of honey, and your favorite chocolate. Melt the chocolate over some hot water and add the ginger. Cook for about one minute and then take off heat. Allow to cool to room temperature. Now add the lemon juice and the honey, because their magic powers are going to get lost, if you put them in the hot mixture.

Make little chocolate toffees out of this mixture and put them in your pocket. The moment you feel queasy, just pop one in your mouth. You may also want to eat one before takeoff, to equalize the air pressure in your ears.

# Making Friends on Trips

I asked a friend what she enjoyed most about her trips, and her immediate answer was making friends. She is a complete extrovert, with plenty of friends of either gender, and she enjoyed making more of them in all corners of the world. That is all very nice, if you are in a country which is comparatively and socially "free," where talking to a man is not considered to be modest or bold.

However, there are many parts of the world, where women traveling alone are considered easy prey. They have no fathers, brothers, or any males around them to protect them foolish women, thinking that they are independent enough.

Unfortunately, such a mindset is still very prevalent in many parts of the world, and that is why a woman alone in such a place may not be safe. You may ask me how I tackle this problem. This is when I leave all my ideas of independence, and feminist liberation, and thankfully take the support and help of any male well-known and trusted friend/colleague/or relative in the area.

They are commanded/commandeered to take me all around the city, shopping, exploring, and all that because after all, I am a guest and visitor to their beautiful city! Or I take another woman friend along with me, especially when I am shopping or exploring. Men do not like shopping as a rule.

That friend has to be "local". And so she knows how best to tackle possible roadside Romeos, shopkeepers inflating their prices, and other potential hazards faced by a woman tourist visiting a place all alone.

Nevertheless, if you find someone, who you think can be a friend, you can talk to him/her. Let them make the first move unless, of course, they are a bit too pushy and want to be your friend, just because you are a tourist and from abroad.

Unfortunately, all over the world, there are societal stereotypes, which have been taught to the children from day go. So, according to these stereotyping lessons, we are under the impression that the French are frivolous, Latinos are more of Casanovas, and are not interested in serious commitments, females from the USA and the UK are easy, and women from the East are repressed.

All these ideas are nonsense. Nevertheless, this is the excuse used by a number of people living in a country in order to impose upon females, especially when they are supposed to be from the West traveling in the East.

One major point to note, please. Most of us are used to living in a free and easy manner in our own particular society, and we subconsciously follow that same pattern when we are traveling somewhere else, in places which may have a different culture than ours.

That is why, if you are used to demonstrations of affection, even hugging your friends, in public, as you do at home, never do that with any friend in any other strange country which you are visiting. Public displays of affection are immediately taken by many people of that country to be a subtle message given out by you that you are available!

Believe it or not, this is what happened to a tourist, who was visiting the Middle East. She was molested, just because she saw one of her colleagues visiting, in that same city. She had not seen him for a really long time, and she gave a whoop of joy, and hugged him. And then because he had some time free, she invited him to lunch at the nearby restaurant where she laughed, giggled, smiled and was extremely charming.

A couple of hours later she was assaulted at night, because the people who had seen this public display of affection and her subsequent behavior thought that she was not a moral woman. *So she deserved what was coming to her.*

The assailants got off Scot- free, because they explained to the police authorities that she had been seen "soliciting" clients in public and everyone knew that any woman eating a meal all alone in a restaurant in daytime with a man not her husband, especially in their city, was not a "good woman."

I do not want you to get afraid, by these real stories, and not go traveling, because anything can happen. I am just telling you to be a bit careful, sensible, and less effusive. Remember that *In Rome do as the Romeos do,* does not work for women.

## Clothes

This is one point which is very important. Remember to wear the clothes, which are worn by people in the country you are visiting. Try to act like you are a local native. Imagine going in the Middle East, where women are garbed from head to foot, and walking the streets wearing a skimpy T-shirt and short shorts. I am definitely not going to be responsible for your personal and physical safety under such circumstances.

Be sensible. You are not going to a country to show off and declare how prosperous you are, by wearing branded labels which incidentally are not rough and tough!

So if you think you are going to wear Alan Solly, Wills style, Gucci, and Nina Ricci, while visiting dusty streets or crowded places of interest, should not you rather have stayed home and impressed the neighbors instead.

Your clothes should be simple, loosefitting – in case you have to run – and please leave those heels at home. Instead, wear canvas shoes or hiking boots. These should be well broken in.

I remember a trip when father forgot to break in his boots, and within four hours, his feet were wailing away. And that is why we were surprised when he told us that he would rather go boating instead of hiking around the city.

So we ordered a boat and enjoyed the whole day boating on the lake. And then we noticed that father had taken off his boots and was massaging his poor feet, while sitting on the boat's well covered seats and not taking a hand on the oars. It was then we understood the necessity for boating instead of hiking!

You may want to take one good party dress, along with you for some special occasion. You never know.

Now you may want to ask what I keep in my bags, apart from medicines for headache and nausea, two pairs of jeans, three bush shirts, four changes of undergarments, and one extra pair of shoes and socks and one lightweight microfiber towel. These are the basics with which I could travel all over the world at the drop of a hat.

Naturally, my documents include my passport, driving license, medical insurance papers, emergency address for contact, credit card, and a diary where I have noted down the addresses of the embassy, the police, important people to contact, the airport and any other information I think I may need.

Apart from that, my clothes are going to be climate specific. But be ready for emergencies. I remember going for a week's tour in December, to a place where I had lived and where I knew the Decembers were mild. So I did not pick up my heavy woolen overcoat. And naturally, that was the time when that area was hit by a free cold wave.

Ice cream had nothing on me in matters of freezing. Just a sweater and a shawl is definitely not effective when the temperature falls below minus 5°. So I had to buy a "wool" overcoat, at about three times its normal cost. And still that did not prevent me from catching a terrible cold!

So if there is the slightest chance of the weather changing, remember to have extra changes of clothing in your bag, especially during the winter.

But this is going to be extra heavy, you are going to say, especially when you are limited to these many pounds in baggage on a number of airlines.

Let me tell you this rather amusing story. I, father and my brother had decided to go on a trip to the mountains about three decades ago. We had to fly there and we knew that the heavy woolen blankets put in our luggage would be too heavy, – weight restrictions – but we needed them!

So father casually folded the blankets, and put them – one each – over our shoulders. And so we boarded the planes with blanket ponchos, as part of our hand luggage! People must have looked at us askance but we were too innocent to know that people did not travel with blankets wrapped around them! Those were the days!

My normally garb while traveling is a dark-colored full sleeved and loose shirt with lots of pockets. And either canvas slacks, flannels or corduroys, because jeans are not very comfortable in which to sleep!

As for my shoes, I have knee length flying boots with sheepskin lining inside. Wonderful for the cold weather. Also, these flying boots are so roomy that you can put things inside them! These things include a packet in which I have my emergency stock of money, and a lighter. Also, one of these boots have a commando knife. It is rather heavy, but I have got used to lugging it around. It gives me a feeling of security, these three decades of traveling. I set up this traveling uniform when I was at college.

It was 10 hours run away from my home, and at the age of 15, my father told me that I was brave enough and independent enough to travel to college all alone. That was because he had brought me up since childhood to enjoy traveling and think of it as a great adventure.

This was in the 80s, and at a time, when women did not move out much all alone from their homes without plenty of family members – male – accompanying them. Somehow, I never noticed anything unusual in the fact that I was traveling alone, possibly because of grandfather's sheathed commando knife- issued to him during the Second World War – tucked in my flying boots, which had been "borrowed" from my uncle!

So you may say, did I get an opportunity to use "my" commando knife, ever. Fortunately, no, never in personal defense, except for cutting up apples and guavas on the way to college and after that, to other places in job-related tours.

Philistine, you may say, that is almost as bad as using precious gem diamonds to cut glass! But that is how life should be lived!

As for a head and face covering, I use a long scarf and baseball cap. That is enough to keep one from getting sunburned and also prevents bleaching of the exposed hair in the hard tropical sun!

# Conclusion

This book may have given you some interesting tips and techniques on how you can enjoy trips, all on your own and keep safe. Many of these tips are based on experience and are definitely based on common sense.

Remember when you are going out on a trip, especially when you are making new friends, remember this innate rule which works for women. Smart women know that life is a balance of luck and good old-fashioned risk-taking. So use your intuition, which is going to save you often.

Trips and holidays can be the start of a brand-new interesting stage of your life. This is a time when you are going to a much your senses in the many joys that the world around you is going to offer

Do not shut out the possibility of beauty and happiness which is the birthright of everyone out there. You have already made a decision to take good care of yourself over the holidays. Remember to plan for relaxation. Pace yourself and take your time in enjoying your surrounding.

It is no fun taking a relaxing holiday, where you exhaust yourself in activities 24 /7!

And remember when you are booking your stay at a hotel, call the hotel directly. Remember to ask about special offers and deals. If they are anxious for your business, they are going to give you the best deals and offers in order to tempt you to stay there and possibly become a long time client.

So enjoy life, live it king-size, Live Long and Prosper!

# Author Bio

**Dueep Jyot Singh** is a Management and IT Professional who managed to gather Postgraduate qualifications in Management and English and Degrees in Science, French and Education while pursuing different enjoyable career options like being an hospital administrator, IT,SEO and HRD Database Manager/ trainer, movie , radio and TV scriptwriter, theatre artiste and public speaker, lecturer in French, Marketing and Advertising, ex-Editor of Hearts On Fire (now known as Solstice) Books Missouri USA, advice columnist and cartoonist, publisher and Aviation School trainer, ex-moderator on Medico.in, banker, student councilor ,travelogue writer … among other things!

One fine morning, she decided that she had enough of killing herself by Degrees and went back to her first love -- writing. It's more enjoyable! She already has 48 published academic and 14 fiction- in- different- genre books under her belt.

When she is not designing websites or making Graphic design illustrations for clients , she is browsing through old bookshops hunting for treasures, of which she has an enviable collection – including R.L. Stevenson, O.Henry, Dornford Yates, Maurice Walsh, De Maupassant, Victor Hugo, Sapper, C.N. Williamson, "Bartimeus" and the crown of her collection- Dickens "The Old Curiosity Shop," and "Martin Chuzzlewit" and so on… Just call her "Renaissance Woman" ) - collecting herbal remedies, acting like Universal Helping Hand/Agony Aunt, or escaping to her dear mountains for a bit of exploring, collecting herbs and plants, and trekking.

Check out some of the other JD-Biz Publishing books

Gardening Series on Amazon

# Health Learning Series

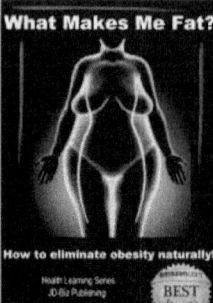

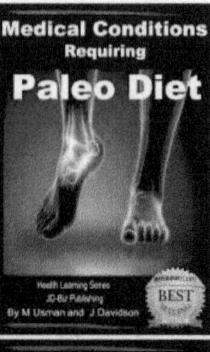

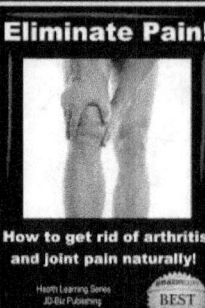

# Amazing Animal Book Series

# Learn To Draw Series

# How to Build and Plan Books

# Entrepreneur Book Series

Our books are available at

1. Amazon.com

2. Barnes and Noble

3. Itunes

4. Kobo

5. Smashwords

6. Google Play Books

# Publisher

JD-Biz Corp

P O Box 374

Mendon, Utah 84325

http://www.jd-biz.com/

Mendon Cottage Books

P O Box 374, Mendon Utah 84325

Mendon Cottage Books

www.ingramcontent.com/pod-product-compliance
Lightning Source LLC
Chambersburg PA
CBHW071130280526
45787CB00003B/1227